# Musings of a Gen X Monkey

# Musings of a Gen X Monkey

Lisa A. Passmore

Copyright © 2024 by Lisa A. Passmore

All rights reserved. No part of this publication may be reproduced, distributed, or transmitted in any form or by any means, including photocopying, recording, or other electronic or mechanical methods, without the prior written permission of the publisher, except in the case of brief quotations embodied in critical reviews and certain other non-commercial uses permitted by copyright law.

ISBN 978-1-62806-430-8  (print | paperback)

Library of Congress Control Number 2024920342

Published by Salt Water Media
29 Broad Street, Suite 104
Berlin, MD 21811
www.saltwatermedia.com

Cover image by the author
Interior images by the author

## Dedication

Rachel, thank you for choosing me.

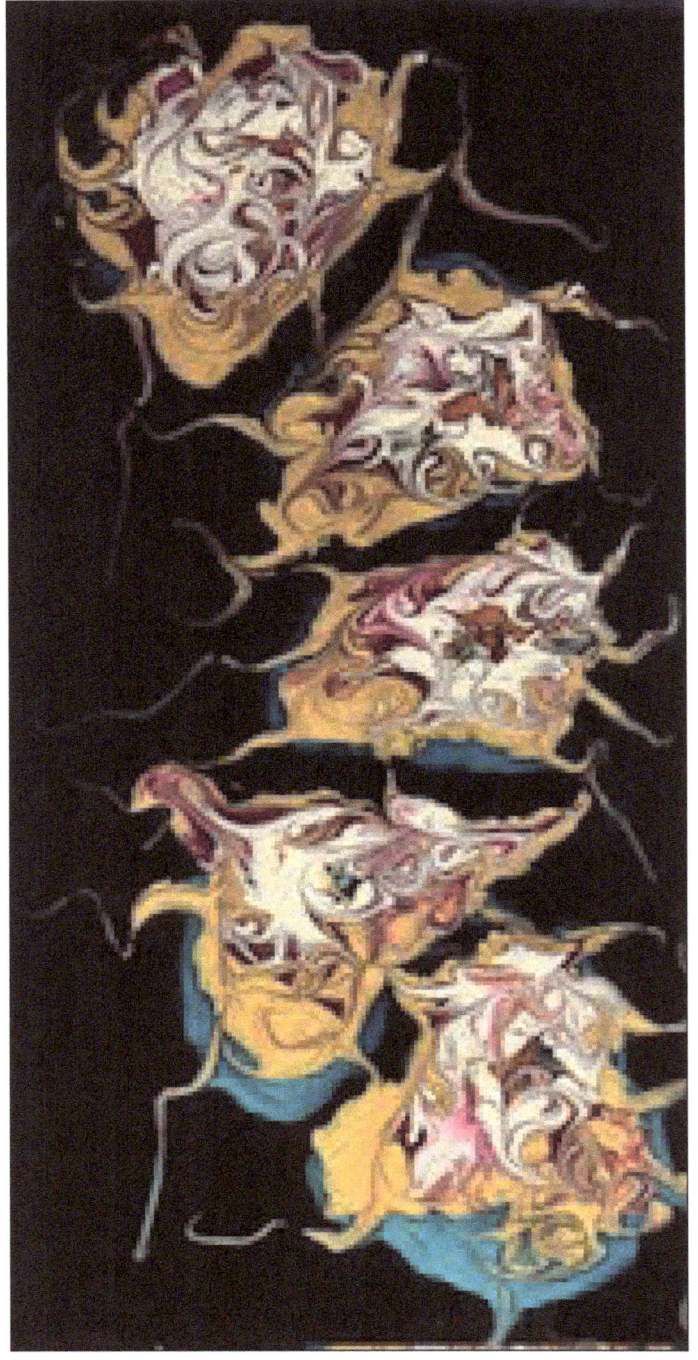

## Contents

| | |
|---|---|
| Daughter's Eyes | 12 |
| Surprise | 15 |
| Baby | 16 |
| Daughter | 19 |
| Creativity | 20 |
| Escape | 23 |
| Dreams | 23 |
| Alphabet | 24 |
| Rachel | 27 |
| Autumn | 27 |
| Ice | 27 |
| I am | 28 |
| Transformation | 31 |
| Cecil Rides the Train | 32 |
| Satisfaction | 32 |
| Leaves | 32 |
| Employment | 35 |
| Profession | 36 |
| Promise | 39 |
| Hate | 39 |
| Snow | 39 |
| FEAR | 40 |
| Music | 40 |
| Empty | 40 |

| | |
|---|---|
| No Vacancy | 42 |
| I am More | 42 |
| The Circle of My Life | 43 |
| Water | 43 |
| Truth | 45 |
| Dragonfly | 46 |
| Love | 48 |
| Confusion | 49 |
| Trust | 51 |
| Pain | 51 |
| Trauma | 51 |
| The Recipe of Me | 52 |
| Am I Enough? | 54 |
| Divorce | 55 |
| Insecure | 57 |
| Guardian Angels | 57 |
| Less Like You | 58 |
| Imposter Syndrome | 61 |
| Shadows and Light | 62 |
| Revelation | 65 |
| Grandsons | 66 |
| Ocean | 66 |
| Trilogy | 66 |
| Anticipation | 69 |
| Spirituality | 69 |

*Poems*

### Daughter's Eyes

On the day he died, she felt pain
The doctor could not find the source
Of deceit

They had waited for news to come
Every day became the last day
To weep

Her innocence was compromised.
When he did not appear to her
For protection

Fantasy became her way out
Dreams would become her way to cope
And escape

The pain would slowly diminish
When she knew he was in her heart
And soul

When his voice was clear through the storm
Deep and safe above the din of
Her suffering

He revealed himself at night
Through her movie dreams as a knight
In Armor

And brought her from darkness to light
As only the dead can do through
Her eyes

### *Surprise*

When I look at her, I feel joy
And safe, knowing she will be loved
By him

They have already made a life
Together with peace, joy, and love
Real love

She does not let him get away
With anything that makes her mad
Or sad

He respects her love of life and
He shares her meaningful love of
Skin ink

They work in a way that should be
Celebrated and seen for the
Beauty

Because he trusts her to show him
The world is a place of wide
Open spaces

And the addition of the babes
Will only serve to increase the
Happy

Place they are creating within
The harsh world of reality
Surprise!

## *Baby*

A
Baby
Creates
Delicious
Energy
For
Grandmothers
Having
Impish
Joy
Keeping
Life
More
Nonsensical
Or
Paradoxically
Quiet
Reserving
Sleep
Time
Unchecked
Visually
Whilst
Examining
Your
Zygote!

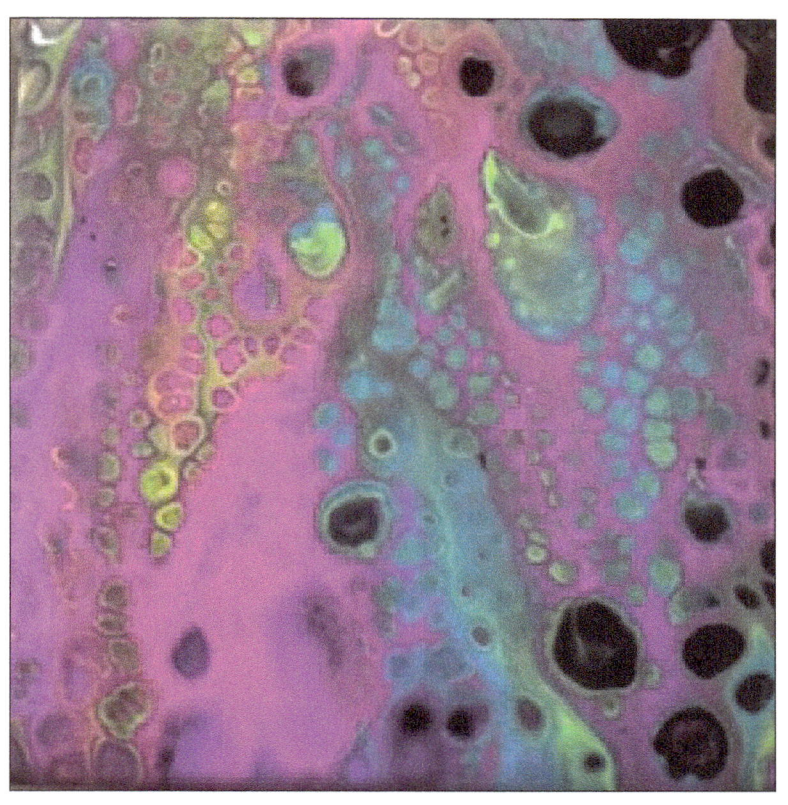

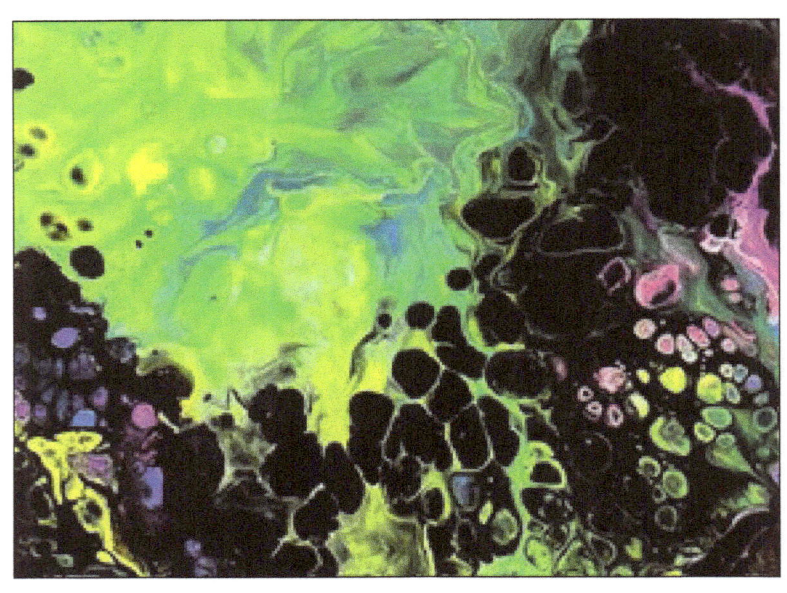

## *Daughter*

A daughter
Brings Joy and
Craziness into a
Delightfully preposterous
Energy
Filled
Game we all
Have to live and play
In
Joy and
Kindness
Live in
Mother and Daughter
Never
Open to
Parting
Quotes are
Rarely
Spoken and
Tough
Understanding
Voices
When
Exacerbating
Your
Zen

## Creativity

A
Beginning
Conjured through
Divine intervention
Exemplifies
Fiery passion and quiets the
Gaslighting
Heard
In times when
Justice is
Killed and
Lit on fire
Murdering her
Noble and
Open soul
Preparing her
Quietly for
Rebirth and
Starting a new
Transformation
Under the
Voracious and
Watchful
Expressions of her
Yearning ancestors
Zeal

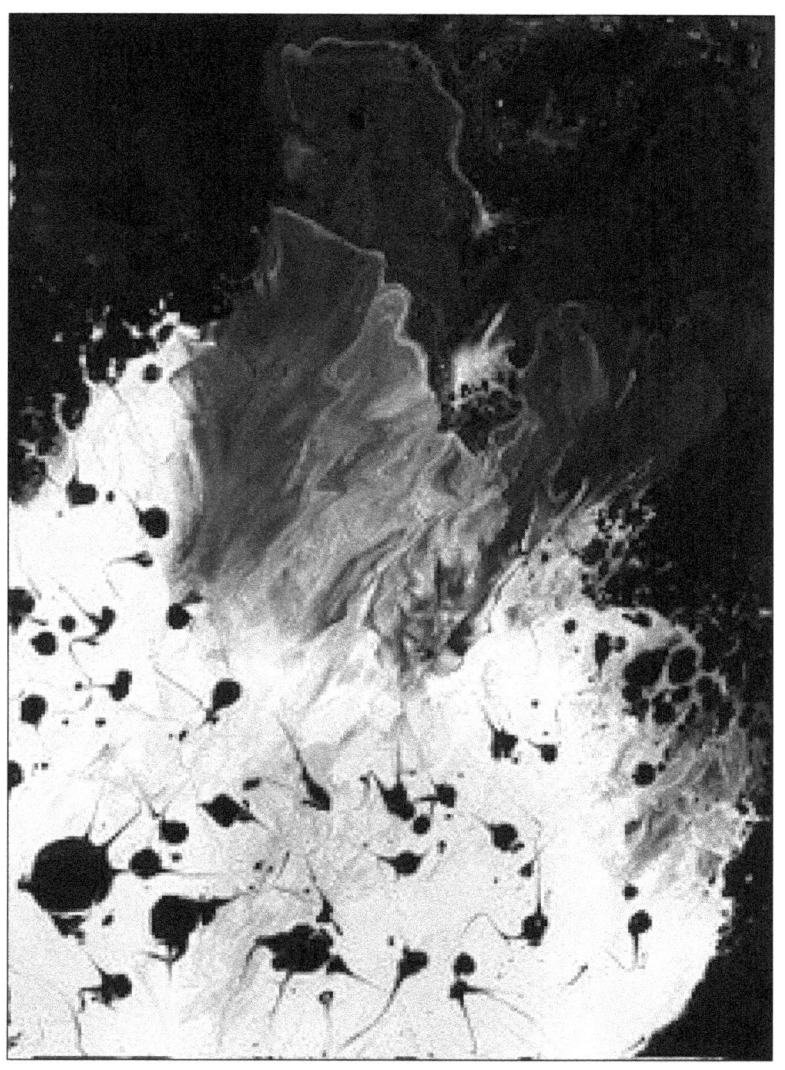

### *Escape*

The full moon rises and the ghosts appear
I try to see through the glass veneer
But I cannot see because of the past
And my soul escapes my mouth so fast
That I fear the skeletons will fall from the hole
Where everyone will see what I don't want them to know
My past I cannot escape
Their mouths agape
It is too much to bear
People stop and stare
At me when I walk through the door
I just want to fall through the floor.

### *Dreams*

I want to go far
Where my life seems to go on
And my dreams come true
To run on the beach with love
And write until the day's done.

## Alphabet

A little girl walks down the street
Because she does not have a name
Chatty in a way that is not normal
Doing special things
Evaluating everything she sees
Friends are in short supply
Going to school is her goal
Having a normal life is not possible
Is it?
Just in time, he sat on the bus
Kisses on the first night
Love comes as a surprise
Magic came into her life
Never did she think he would leave
One night was the undoing
Peace could not be found
Quietly, she sat outside to wait
Remembering the letters he sent
She was not good-looking or smart enough
Tough she became
Until she saw her eyes
Vulnerable was her new feeling
Wonderment at every turn
Xray when she skated
Years go by and she heals
Zeal for the life she has found

### Rachel

Rachel is an
Angel who has
Chosen
Her mother and
Eternally
Loved

### Autumn

The trees bend with angst
As leaves turn brown and gold
And the fierce wind blows
Smells of burned leaves soothes
Windows are open at night
And sleep comes to her.

### Ice

Snow falls on the tree.
Ice comes with the rain cleanses
And the world sparkles.

## *I am*

I am creative and dark
I wonder about the expanding Universe
I hear music when I see light
I see blue and black and red and purple
I want a full life
I am creative and dark
I pretend I am something I may become
I feel light as a feather
I touch the heart of the unloved
I worry the secrets are kept
I cry for the damages done
I am creative and dark
I understand love is finite
I say I am
I dream of wind and sand
I try not; I do
I hope for an end to the pressure
I am creative and dark

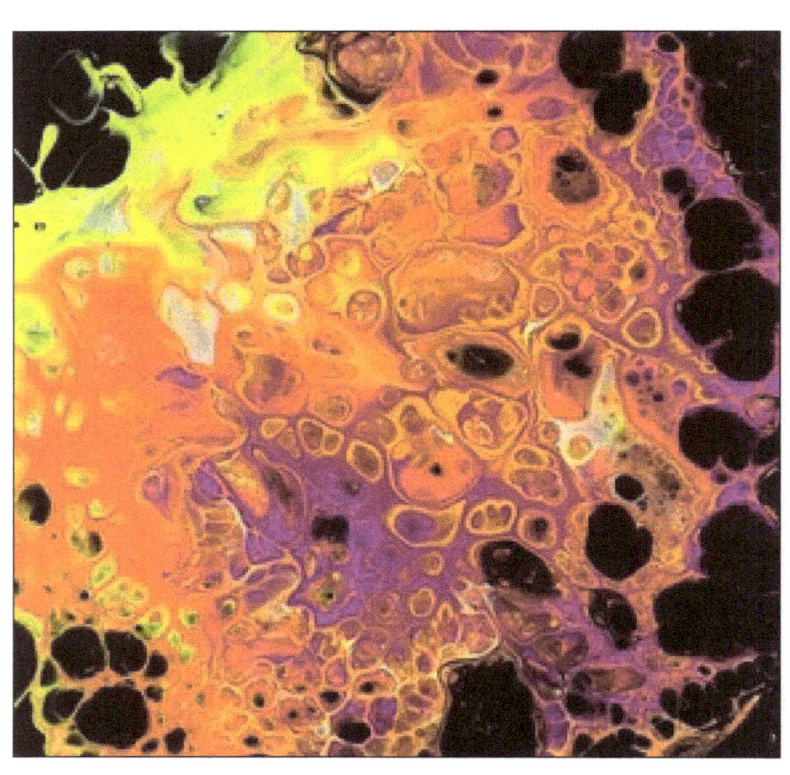

## Transformation

The pain and sadness are waning
Days and nights are full of love
And when I feel myself refraining
From the gentleness, I close my eyes and look above.

I find the guidance of my angels
They lift me up and cradle me gently in their arms
where I can rest peacefully in their eyes of hazel
and laugh realizing their charms

Are a part of my DNA; deep in my core.
I feel the shift in my heart and soul
and every decision I make becomes more
like the human I am supposed to be and console

the damaged little girl
who is indeed an important part of this world.

### Cecil Rides the Train

He floated on the train as I watched
His threadbare wings were notched
With the grace only the aged can possess
Where he was going, I could not guess
But those who were lucky enough to witness him fly
Found their souls filled and a need to cry
As he gracefully lived out the last of his days
His tattered wings filtered the sun's rays
And created a work of art on the floor
Then at the next stop he flew out the door.

### Satisfaction

Will there ever be a time I will be able to stay
At a place worth the pay
Makes me feel I can play
In the sandbox and not get the sand flung in my eye
And not have to feel like a baby and cry?

### Leaves

The autumn leaves cry
As they drift softly to die
And mix with the Earth.

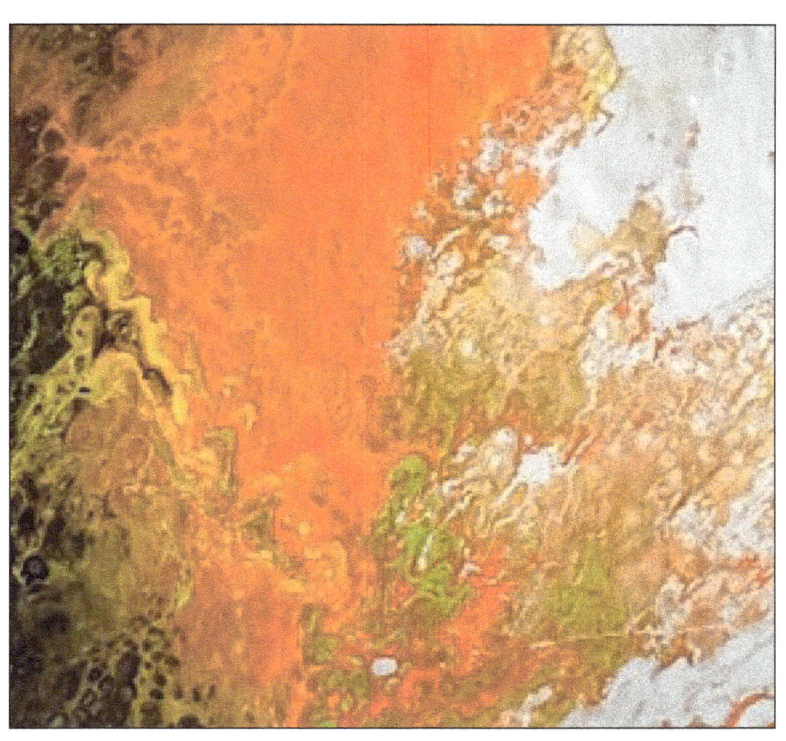

*Employment*

Angst
Boring
Callous
Detrimental
Envious
Fake
Girls
Hate
Insipid
Jealousy
Knowledge
Limit-setting
Managers
Nosocomial
Oppressive
Palliative
Questioning
Reasonable
Stymied
Trolls
Unbridled
Verity
Wishes
Xray
Yearning
Zoo

## Profession

Able-minded and strong
Because of the trials and errors
Coming from the childhood
Dreams that never died
Except for love
Finding that is proving to be of
Great and
Heated
Imagination.
Just because I won't believe in love doesn't mean I don't. I
Keep
Looking for it.
Matriculation has become a replacement for the
Nearness of another soul
Owning up to a
Pretty life that
Quietly tears the heart to shreds
Remembering the dreams that
Sometimes reveal themselves in the shadows of
Thoughts once
Universally accepted but
Vanish as quickly as they come.
When the tears fall jagged like the cuts of an
Xacto knife
Youth becomes a
Zombie.

## Promise

People are basically uninformed.
Reading material who have been simplified
Once the world realizes things that really
Matter
I will be there to
See they are
Enlightened.

## Hate

Happiness is the
Antithesis of
The way I do not want to live
Every day.

## Snow

Flakes glide to the ground
Where they gather into drifts
And melt with the sun.

## FEAR

Feelings that never
Enlighten
A
Real person


## Music

Music is the sanity flowing through my veins
And takes me to a safe place
And away from the vagaries of life
That tend to weigh the soul down like an anchor
Music lifts the weight and turns it into atoms absorbed by
my brain.


## Empty

Everything feel like
My
Poor brain will pop out of my
Tiny skull
Yelling.

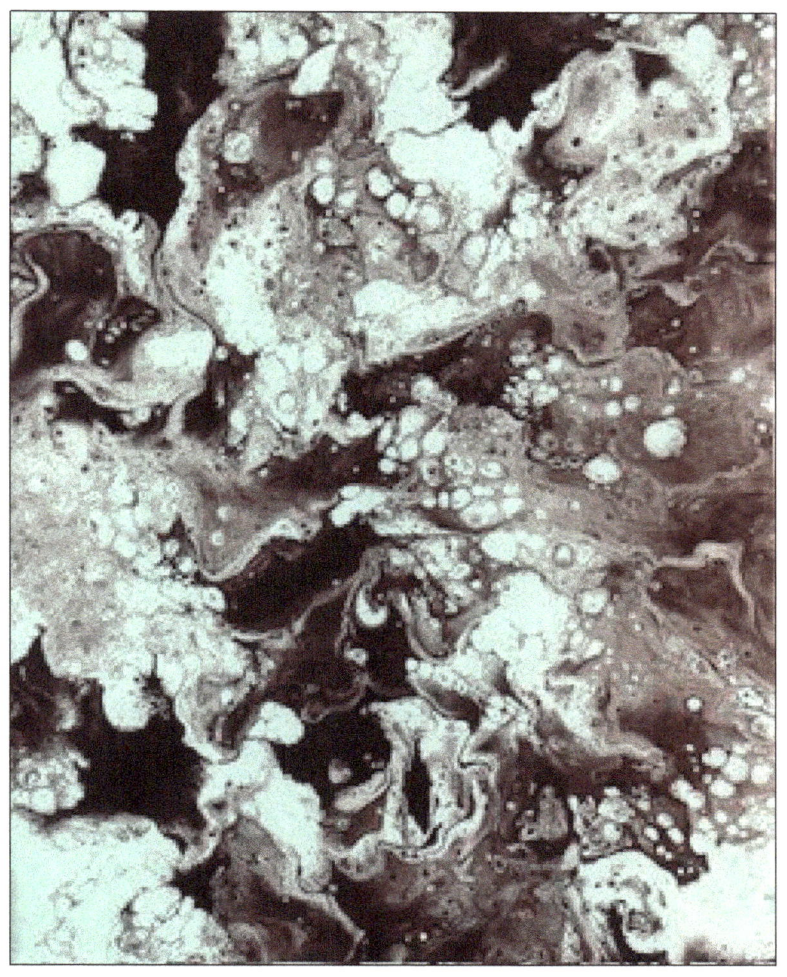

## No Vacancy

There is no vacancy.
There is only room for one.
And that one has stolen my heart
And I don't know what I will do when she finally realizes what
A fraud I am.


## I am More

I am complex and pervasive
I wonder if I will ever be satisfied
I hear voices in juxtaposition
I see myself on a cloud
I want love
I am complex and pervasive
I pretend to live a life in a film noir
I feel the tingling of my soul
I touch the mind of my ancestors
I worry about failure
I cry when I think of Face
I am complex and pervasive
I understand where my anger originates
I say I am
I dream I one day can make my happiness
I try not. I do
I hope I am worth the trouble for someone special
I am complex and pervasive.

## The Circle of My Life

Life is cyclic; what goes 'round
comes 'round when you least expect
the sorrows turn into lessons;
lessons become transformation;
transformation allows new insight
into the person you are to be.
Always remember who you were before
because she was the one who saved you from
yourself when there was no hope or light or love.
This brand new joy fills the space in life's circle

## Water

Water offers peace
I sit on my couch and smile.
It has absorbed my trauma.

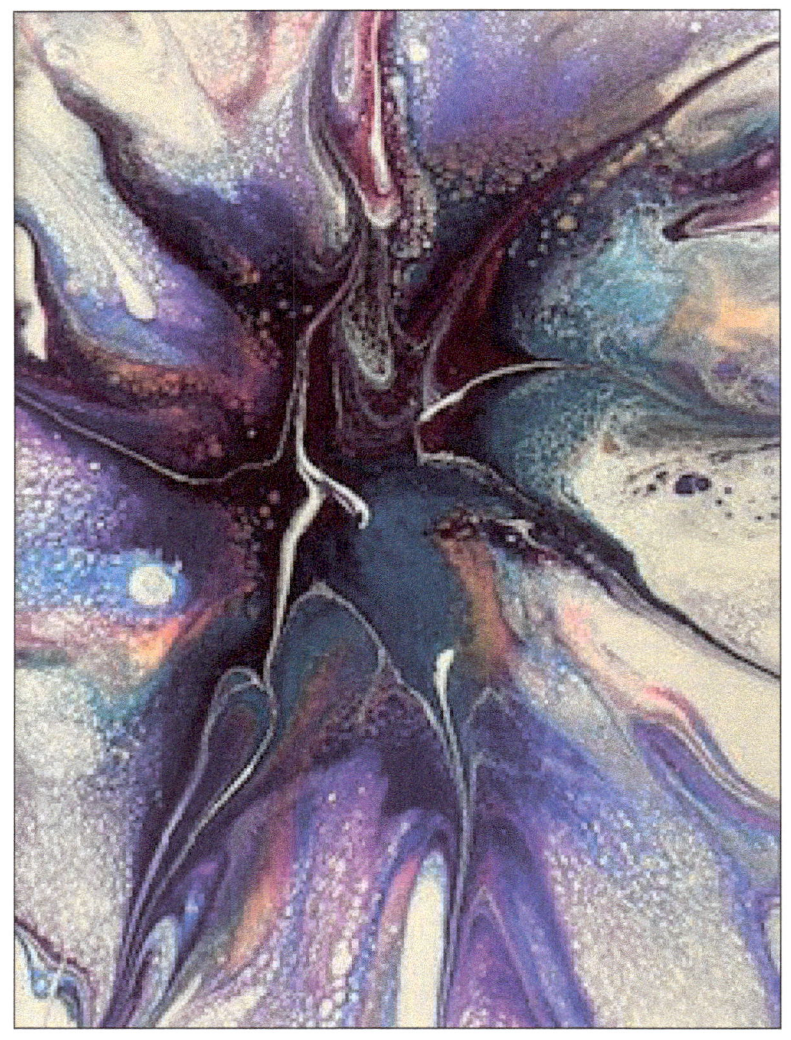

## *Truth*

She opened her eyes and felt warmth
Like a blanket wrapped around her
Cool soul.

The bright lights shining down on her
Like the sun on a summer's day
Lifting her

Spirit as high as the eagle
Floating on a current of air
Ever up

further and further from the ground
where the rare air held her captive
against

the wind gently caressing her
rapidly beating heart until
she fell

to the icy slab of concrete;
the previous bright lights now dark
as night.

She closed her eyes against the truth
That she no longer walks among
The living.

Forever trapped under the ground
Awaiting return to the earth
She sighed.

## *Dragonfly*

You now come to me as a dragonfly.
For so many years, I could not mourn
you because I was only surviving.
The medium saw you standing in front of other family,
But I did not recognize your soul.
And I will forever feel the sorrow.

You were the blanket wrapped around me in my sorrow.
Then one day, years later, you came to me as a dragonfly.
I immediately recognized your soul
And the part of me holding onto the need to mourn
Transitioned to my new role in my family.
And moved to thriving rather than surviving.

You are my guardian angel and surviving
Without you still brings me sorrow
But knowing you are now with family
On earth playfully flitting about as a dragonfly
I no longer feel the need to mourn
Your beautiful soul.

I feel your soul
As it floats down to me on the days I'm surviving;
Diving deep in shadows to the place I mourn
Where I no longer need to feel the sorrow.
Because you, my dragonfly
Are inextricably tied to family.

Life is complicated and family

Communicates through my soul.
The transparent wings of a dragonfly
Moving gracefully through the humid air surviving
Never spreading sorrow
And no longer feeling the need to mourn.

So much time wasted; dying to mourn.
You cannot be a part of the earth family
And the sorrow

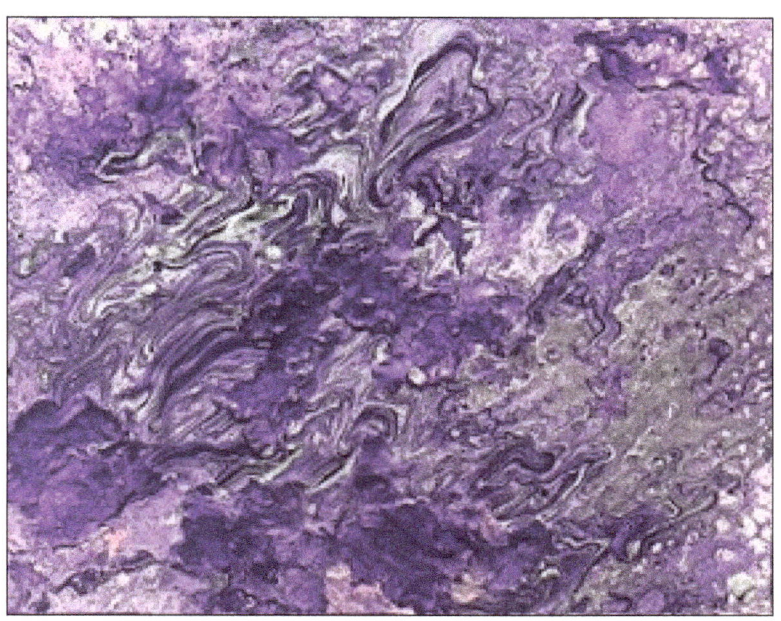

## Love

How do we get past
The trauma and pain of love
When they are heartless
And our pain feeds their need
To decimate and destroy?
Am I enough?

Is it enough
To let go of the past
Before the emotions begin to destroy
What we know of love?
How can we trust ourselves to know what we need
So we don't become as heartless?

The ancestral line cannot all be heartless.
Perhaps only one was enough
To break down the human need
To forget the past
And rebuild a foundation of love
Instead of their intrinsic need to destroy.

How does one become an instrument meant to destroy?
Do they start or end heartless?
And only know the opposite of love?
Isn't it enough
To let go of the past
And feed the need?

To do and be better; the need

To break a pure and innocent soul down and destroy
And decimate to the point there is no past
And morph into another heartless
Shell where there will never be enough
Love?

What is love?
Something we want or what we need?
Is that enough
To obfuscate our Machiavellian machination to destroy
The very innocence and render humanity heartless
And circle back to the past?

The human need to love and destroy in equal measure
Will surely outweigh the need of the heartless
Incomplete human whose past is not enough.

### Confusion

The need consumes me
Causing you pain is my goal
But you have no heart
Pain brings you satisfaction
I am left dazed and confused

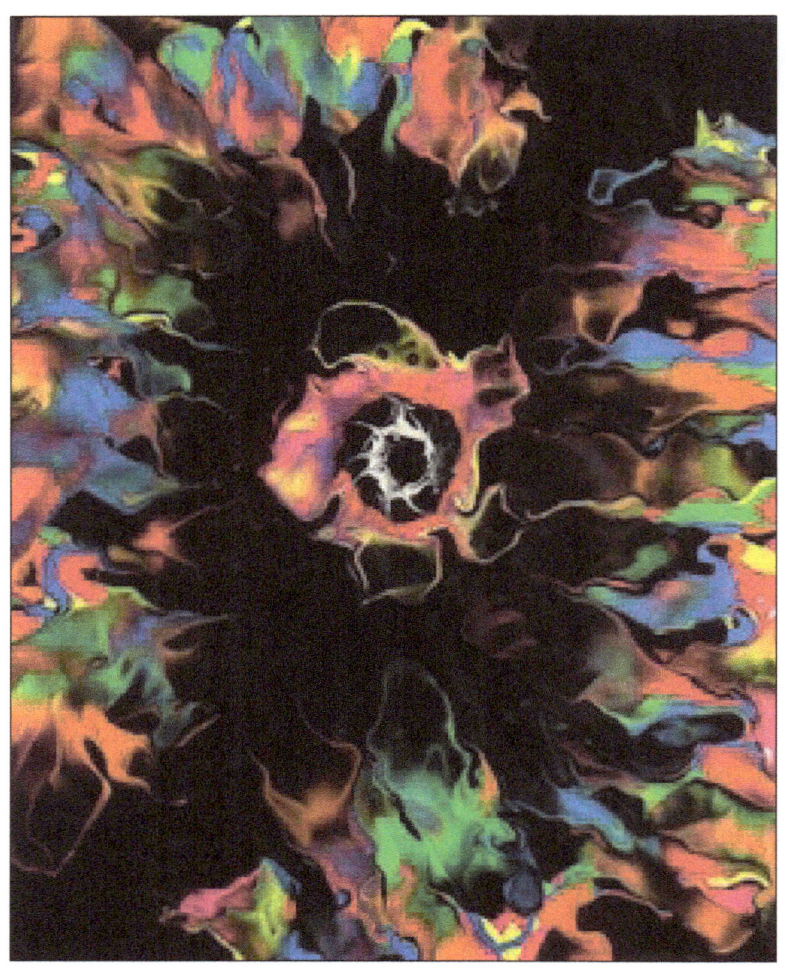

### *Trust*

Truth always finds a way
Right back to the
Unsuspecting partner who
Suspects the one who does not
Deserve
Trust.

### *Pain*

Please
Allow
Instant
Numbness

### *Trauma*

Those who are supposed to
Rear us
Are the ones who
Usually end up
Maiming our souls
And hearts.

## The Recipe of Me

You're a little salty; pick another spice.
The way you talk and walk and think is not like a proper girl.
Don't you know you're supposed to be nice?

The way you look at them seems you are filled with ice.
Your hair does not shine in the light nor curl.
You're a little salty; pick another spice.

Your thousand-yard stare holds them like a vice.
But they want you to be as shiny as a pearl.
Don't you know you're supposed to be nice?

How many times do I have to repeat myself? Twice?
Spinning myself so fast I feel the need to hurl.
You're a little salty; pick another spice.

Yet I continue to roll myself around like dice.
I wish I could find the impetus to twirl.
Don't you know you're supposed to be nice?

No, you don't have to remind me thrice.
My ingredients come together in a delicious swirl.
You're a little salty; pick another spice.
Don't you know you're supposed to be nice?

## *Am I Enough?*

Will there ever be a time I will feel I'm enough?
Maybe I am never to be loved
But am here to bring love to the world.
Find the way through the pain
And emerge from the darkness into light
Perhaps in my next life.

Do I get to choose who I become in the next life?
Where I decide, I AM enough.
I get to stand on the stage under a bright light
The audience claps and screams out how much I am loved
I close my eyes and feel no pain
As I give all of myself to the world.

I can picture the madness this next world
Brings to life
Carrying the pain
Of those ancestors who never felt they were enough
And only wanted to be loved
And walk beside one another into the light.

The smoldering sun shines its dim light
Down on what's left of this world
Where inhabitants thought they were loved
Existing in illusions they called life
In the end, all their sacrifices were never enough
Because what was left in the shadows was pain.

What she thought she felt was pain

Forced her eyes open so she could witness the light
And realized she was enough
Because life in this new world
Held surprises she never had in her former life
And found she was loved.

She now knows how it feels to be loved
When she used to only know pain
That kept her going on with her melancholy life
Not realizing she was the reason there was no light
Shining down on her because she held the world
In her heart where she was enough.

To be loved and feel the light; living the pain inflicted
On the world is enough for her in this new life.

## Divorce

Daring to move on from
Incomplete humans often demand a
Very high price paid by the
One who was wronged and forces us to
Rip out our hearts and
Calm our souls. In the
End we heal.

*Insecure*

Insane
Numb
Sensations
Escape
Causation
Unspoken
Real
Ending.

**Guardian Angels**

They die.
Then appear in dreams.
I don't know what you want.
Will you kindly show me the way?
I'll go.

## Less Like You

I need to find a way to be more like me and less like you.
I look in the mirror and my reflection is cliché.
I transform a little more every day.

To be bolder and stand out, I got my first tattoo.
What was once an insult I now understand what you were trying to portray.
I need to find a way to be more like me and less like you.

Exercise, dieting, fasting to starvation are all the methods I tried to pursue.
In the end, all I felt was full of dismay.
I transform a little more every day.

Bringing her into this world was a chance for me to renew
The sense I am more than what I weigh.
I need to find a way to be more like me and less like you.

No longer believing I am askew
Myself I no longer betray
I transform a little more every day.

Every day feels like I am born anew
And no longer feel I am on display.
I need to find a way to be more like me and less like you.
I transform a little more every day.

## *Imposter Syndrome*

Insecurity
Many
People
Often
See
The
External
Rational
Skin
Yet
Never
Do I
Rely
On
My
Exoskeleton

## *Shadows and Light*

I survive between the shadows and the light
Always moving somewhere no one can detect the devastation
I thrive between wanting the roar of the spotlight and the quiet of isolation.

Sometimes I get so tired I want to give up the fight.
And protect myself from further annihilation.
I survive between the shadows and the light

I revel in the moments I feel powerfully and abundantly bright.
And I soak in the glorious rays of the sun.
I thrive between wanting the roar of the spotlight and the quiet of isolation.

The thought I will disappear gives me a fright.
And all I can do is speak aloud words of consolation.
I survive between the shadows and the light

Then there are the days I just might
Dive back under the covers of matriculation.
I thrive between wanting the roar of the spotlight and the quiet of isolation.

The need to book an adventure on the very next flight
Forces me to bring myself back to earth feeling like an aberration.
I survive between the shadows and the light
I thrive between wanting the roar of the spotlight and the quiet of isolation.

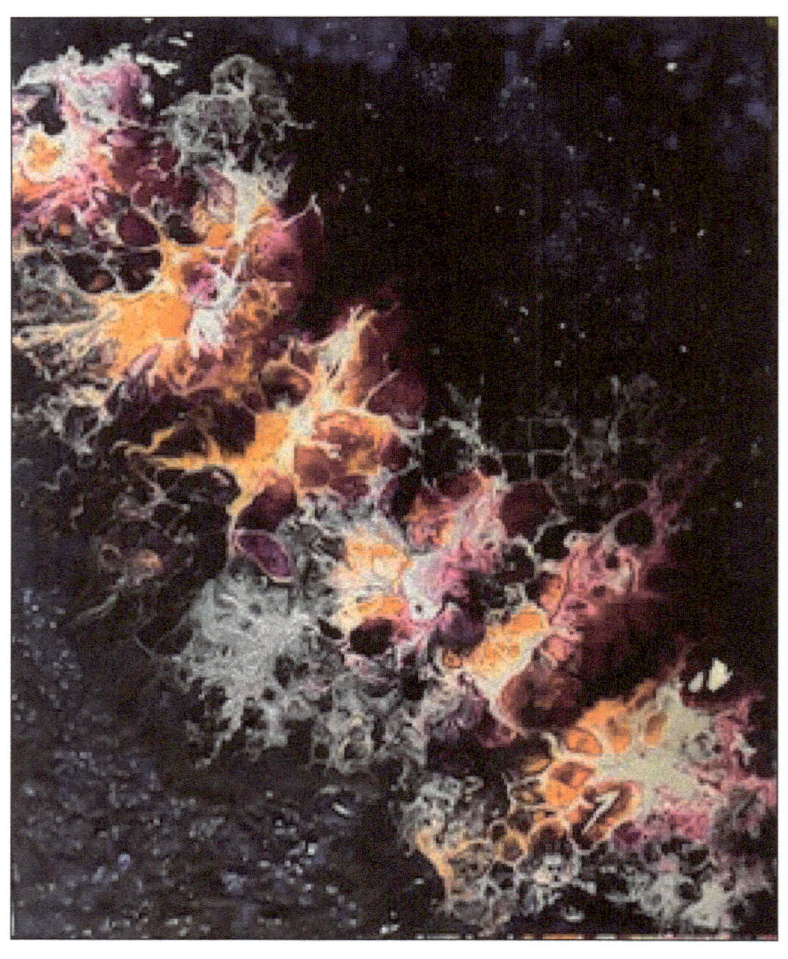

## *Revelation*

I did not know what I did not know; until I knew.
The formative years were replete with comfortable discomfort.
When the discomfort turned to pain and tears were the balm
I found what I needed, a well-lit path to the truth.

This comfortable discomfort followed me through my formative years.
As I moved from relationship to relationship.
The well-lit path revealed my truth
And gave me the strength to dive deep into the shadows.

Moving from relationship to relationship
placed another clue to solving the mystery
and revealed the shadows where my strength cowered.
Every day gives me more insight.

The mystery is being solved day by day.
Demonstrating I found, I knew what I did not know.
Insight is coming to me in waves every day.
morphed into the balm the tears where once only discomfort.

### Grandsons

Their love
Is powerful
Their hugs hold light magic
Their eyes tell the story of me
My heart.

### Ocean

I fear the dark depth
The shadows of the water
Hide shades of darkness
The expanse holds night creatures
Or are they just my nightmares?

### Trilogy

Little girl sits shy
Adolescent folds broken
Elder sighs deeply
They are all pieces of me
As I lay remembering.

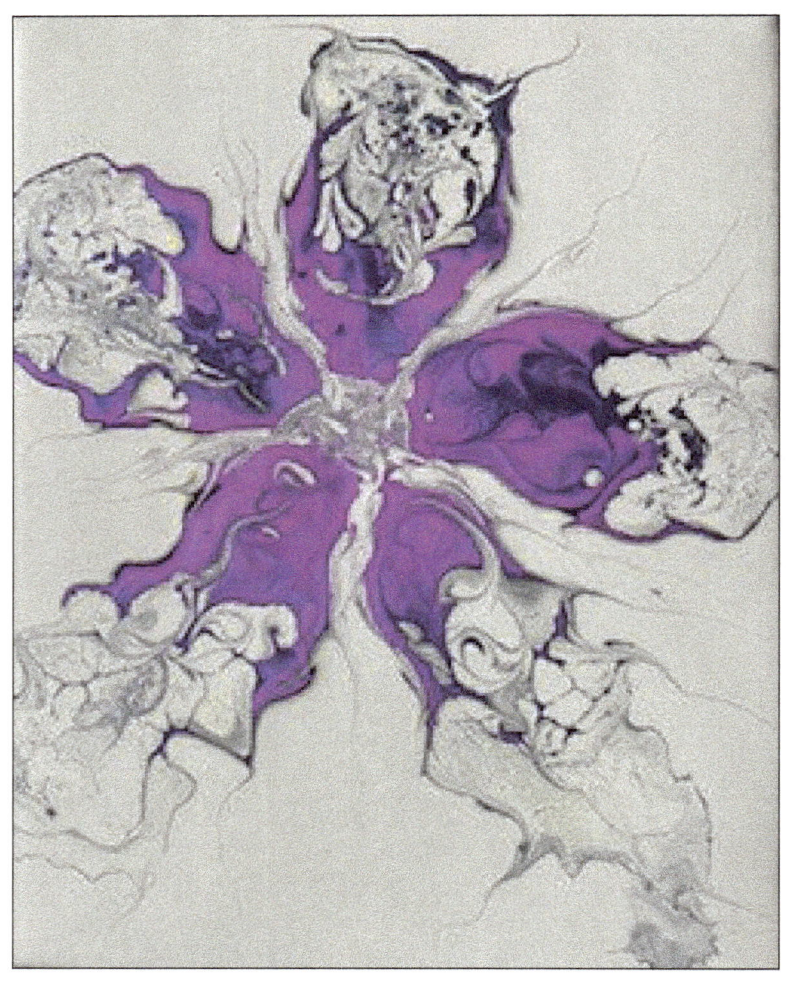

### *Anticipation*

Soulmate
The cards tell me
One day, I will be loved
And accepted just as I am
Enough.

### *Spirituality*

I am.
Tasked with breaking
Generational lies
And curses never meant for me
Ready.

## About the Author

Dr. Lisa Passmore is a Florida resident who is healing and becoming a better citizen of the Universe. She has spent the last 20 years as a nurse cultivating her creativity in various ways including photography, writing, and painting. Lisa's love for her two grandsons, daughter, and son-in-law inspire her every day.

www.ingramcontent.com/pod-product-compliance
Lightning Source LLC
Chambersburg PA
CBHW050817090426
42736CB00022B/3486